HOMEWORK SORTED!

Kate Brookes

Developed in association with

from *The Guardian*

HODDER
Wayland

a division of Hodder Headline Limited

Published in Great Britain 2002 by Hodder Wayland,
an imprint of Hodder Children's Books

10 9 8 7 6 5 4 3 2 1

A catalogue record for this book is available from the
British Library.

ISBN: 0 7502 41721

Hodder Children's Books
a division of Hodder Headline Limited
338 Euston Road
London NW1 3BH

Printed and bound in Great Britain

CONTENTS

INTRODUCTION

Homework Sorted! has been written to help you manage your homework so that you stay on top, in control and stress-free. It shares loads of tips for maximising your marks and getting the job done right first time. There's also the low-down on making a computer your best homework buddy!

Whether you like it or not, homework is regarded as part of the normal school day and is here to stay! So, if you can't avoid homework, then finding the speediest, least painful and most successful way through it should be high on your wish-list.

Not all bad news

Most of you are happy to do homework in your favourite subjects, or to do homework that is different to your class work – designing a poster for art, getting your mates together to write and rehearse a script for drama, for example. You get stuck into these pieces of homework because you feel confident about what's to be done, know you can do it quickly, know that you'll get good marks, or suspect that it could be a bit of fun. *Homework Sorted!* will help you feel equally confident, efficient, successful and enthused about **all** your homework, not just your best subjects.

It's a partnership

Homework Sorted! won't make you hard-working, can't provide ready-made answers to all homework tasks, or make boring tasks exciting. Nor will it make homework go away. But if you take on board its advice, put its tips into practice and establish a homework routine, you will be moving in homework's fast lane. At the same time, you'll be gathering knowledge, skills, marks, praise and a well-deserved sense of achievement.

Don't overdo it!

No one knows for certain whether homework is good for you. Some experts say a little bit is a good idea, and many agree that being given too much or spending too much time on your homework can have negative consequences. Even though these doubts exist, you're bound to be given homework today so here are four good reasons to knuckle down and get it done:

1. *Homework Sorted!* will show you how to spend less time on your homework without losing marks.

2. If the homework routine becomes less of a chore, then your attitude to homework, school and studying in general will improve.

3. If you do your homework and do it well, you can expect respect from your teachers and zero grief.

4. With a good homework record, you might be able to influence what your teachers assign as homework. Now, that's an interesting idea!

Credit where credit is due

The original inspiration and much of the information for this soon-to-be-indispensable book came from **learn.co.uk**, the award-winning education website backed by *The Guardian*. And so, huge thanks to Andrew Moore who researched and wrote the **Homework guide**.

To read the original material in full (especially the comprehensive sections on using computers and the Internet for your homework), go to: **www.learn.co.uk/ homework/**

CHAPTER 1

HOMEWORK – WHY?

SO, WHAT IS HOMEWORK?

One headteacher, interviewed for a radio programme, said it was "work that is done at home". This wasn't very clever, and wasn't even completely accurate – homework is often done out of the home. Some experts describe homework as tasks which "consolidate, reinforce and extend work in the classroom".

In some ways, the name 'homework' is very old-fashioned, as if there are only two places where you can do work – if it's not school, then it must be at home. More recently we have heard the phrase 'anytime, anywhere learning' which is based on the idea that homework is portable, and you can do it wherever you are. This might seem wonderful or scary – is there nowhere you can escape from work!?

IT'S OFFICIAL!

When a year 1 pupil makes a robot from cereal packets for their homework, they are on official government business. Homework is not something that teachers give out because they feel like it or because they didn't cover everything in class; they are following Government recommendations and guidelines.

The Department for Education and Skills (DfES) says that "homework helps children to develop important skills, in particular those of independent learning". And in order to achieve a level of independent learning, the DfES suggests how much homework you should be doing:

SCHOOL	HOMEWORK YEAR
Years 1 and 2	60 minutes a week
Years 3 and 4	90 minutes a week
Years 5 and 6	30 minutes a day
Years 7 and 8	45–90 minutes a day
Year 9	1–2 hours a day
Years 10 and 11	1.5–2.5 hours a day

QUALITY NOT QUANTITY

The Government is anxious for you to know that the quantity of homework you get isn't half as important as whether it is helping you to learn. They say homework should be:

- well-planned so that you don't have lots on one night and nothing the next.

- realistic in the amount of work to be done and the time it should take.

- clearly organised and explained so that you are in no doubt about what you have to do.

- obviously related to class work.

- not too easy, nor too hard.

- a mixture of 'activities' – reading, writing, planning, researching, making something, etc.

- marked so that you get feedback for your effort and to show that homework is as important as classroom assignments.

- planned so that it can be done outside the home in a library or homework club, for example.

- suited to the needs of individuals.

Your school's homework plans are something that OFSTED inspectors check, so homework is not all fun and games for teacher's either.

HOMEWORK — NO WAY!

You know where your homework comes from and where it should be taking you, but many experts still think homework is a waste of time. Some of the 'down with homework' crowd believe:

1. If parents show no interest in their children's homework, then why should their children.

2. Important work should or will be covered in class. Therefore, homework is not important.

3. It's too easy to cheat at homework, therefore homework can't count for anything.

None of these are valid reasons. Read on to discover why.

Do you have to do it?

The short answer is no. If you really want to avoid homework, you will probably find a way to do so.

Even the Home-School Agreement, which you and a parent sign, and which tells you that homework is as much a part of the school day as maths and science is not legally binding. There's no 'law' that says you have to do homework. But regularly not doing homework could result in you (and possibly a parent) spending quality time with the headteacher!

While homework is made easier if a parent supports your efforts, homework is your responsibility because you are the one who will benefit.

SO, WHY DO IT?

On page 7 there were four reasons for doing homework and here are four more:

1. Homework supports and reinforces class work and gives you a chance to practise skills learned in class. Without this practice you'll never know if you can perform the task and understand the concepts.

2. Homework is different to class work. You can work at your own pace and, best of all, you can do it in your pyjamas while eating popcorn!

3. Homework gives you a chance to show that you're an independent and motivated pupil up for a challenge. That's why sheep don't get homework – they can't act independently!

4. Not doing homework or cheating at it means you are missing out on crucial knowledge and skills for coursework and exams. Cheats in the end only cheat themselves.

CHAPTER 2

WORK SMARTER, NOT HARDER

Given a choice, which sounds like the better deal – labouring painfully over an assignment into the early hours the night before it's due OR spreading the work over a couple of weeks and enjoying nights of cosy kip? You do have a choice between working harder or working smarter!

WHAT'S THE DIFFERENCE?

Work harder

- Late nights

- Work piles up

- Panic attacks

- Frustrated because your homework falls below your ability

- Being creative with excuses

- Hassling mates for help at the last minute

- Feeling constantly under a cloud of 'undone' homework

- Asking for extensions... again!

- Missing out on the fun stuff because you have lots of homework due

Work smarter

- Snuggled down in bed
- In control and on top of your work
- Panic – what's that?
- Happy because your homework demonstrates your ability to do well
- Excuses? – huh!
- Working with mates to share the load
- Walking on sunshine!
- Assignments handed in on time, no sweat!
- Getting loads of the fun stuff

SMART ATTACK

Here is an eight-point strategy to help you conquer homework:

1. Create a homework timetable.

Fix a starting time and a finishing time, bearing in mind the guidelines on page 13. You can do your homework in one sitting (but do take a short break between each item of homework) or spread it over two sessions (one straight after school, the second after supper, for example).

Your timetable should be realistic and allow room for other activities. There's no point pencilling in homework when you should be at drama rehearsals or when you meet your friends in the gym for a sweat session.

ADVICE FROM THE TOP

Create a homework timetable during the first week of term and start using it in the second week!

2. **Write in the timetable when each subject is given homework and when it is due back.**
Teachers aim to give homework on set days and then expect its return on a set day that week or the next. This is not just for their benefit, but to give you a chance to plan your time.

If you're not sure what the homework routine is, check with each subject teacher.

ADVICE FROM THE TOP

Take two photocopies of your timetable. Stick one into your school homework diary and the other in the kitchen so that your family appreciates just how hard you're working. Stick the original timetable near where you do your homework.

3. **On a wall calendar or in your diary, fill in the deadlines for long-term assignments and coursework.**

Also write in when teachers want to check your work-in-progress and when a project is meant to have reached a certain stage. Teachers set these progress dates to help you stay on track, so don't ignore them.

Once these dates are on a calendar, it's easy to spot if two major pieces are due on the same day. You can plan around this conflict or talk to one of your teachers about adjusting a deadline. If you have an early warning of any tests, jot these on the calendar as well.

ADVICE FROM THE TOP

Colour-code each subject so that you can quickly spot each stage of an assignment.

4. *Make a list of regular tasks for each school subject.*

For example, writing a summary of each chapter of a set text as you read it or memorising each new vocabulary list for German as you are given it. Your teachers may not remind you that these regular jobs have to be done, so put the list above your desk, add to it when necessary and always refer to it when doing your homework.

5. **As soon as a piece of homework is set, spend a minute reviewing the question or task.**

Has the teacher specified how many words you should write? Is there a list of resources, materials, reference books or websites? Are there suggestions about how to tackle it and the best place to start? Is the aim of the homework clear and do you know what you should get out of it? Do you know what materials (for example, graph paper) need to be taken home? If not, then ask the teacher NOW!

ADVICE FROM THE TOP

Teachers brim with positive feelings when a student shows intelligent interest in their work. What's intelligent interest? You asking the teacher questions that will help you tackle any topic or task. Try it out for yourself.

You could also ask your teacher what will boost marks – graphs, illustrations, pictures, doing it on a computer, imaginative presentation, quotes, statistics, for example. Checking homework straight away will save a mini panic attack at home later, and pumping the teacher for guidance, hints and tips will save you valuable time.

ADVICE FROM THE TOP

Don't let the teacher get away with setting homework that is vague or too demanding for the amount of time. Talk to your mates and see if they agree, then speak to the teacher and present your case clearly and politely.

6. *Make the task fit the time.*

Some of you take your homework so seriously that it consumes your every working moment. Time/length suggestions from teachers are there for good reasons.

- Assess the time to be spent on the task in proportion to what it contributes to your class assessments or exams. If a project contributes 12.5% to Year 11, for example, then it's worth more effort than an end-of-topic 'revision' quiz.

- Completing a task within a set time or number of words gives you practice in planning and presenting the important and relevant information concisely and clearly.

- Setting limits means that you learn to set boundaries on your research, quickly sussing out what is useful and what is unnecessary or irrelevant.

- Neither teachers nor the Government want you to fill every free hour doing homework. They know you have interests and passions that are equally – and often more – important.

ADVICE FROM THE TOP

For biggish pieces of homework, write down what you have to do in your own words. Once you have a plan, set a time/length limit for each phase of the plan, then get stuck in. A snappy way to remember this is: First, plan your work. Second, work your plan.

7. Reduce the workload.

The bottom line with homework and especially coursework is that you must do it yourself. BUT friends and family can help in lots of ways. Adults can search out books in the library, photocopy sections of useful information, print out websites from a list you have compiled, help you key in or proofread an assignment, and test vocabulary and fact lists. They can also suggest ways of doing something, show you how to work something out, give you ideas and share their opinions.

Friends can share the research for an assignment and then pool what each other has found. The writing up, though, is a solo job where everyone creates a unique piece of work.

ADVICE FROM THE TOP

School libraries are sometimes the last place you think of looking for help, but they should be the first. Unlike a public library that has to meet the needs of a whole community, a school library is just for you. For any major assignment you can bet the school library is well prepared.

8. Hand in quality work every time.

When doing the first draft of a story, don't be tempted to overlook the dodgy spelling, iffy punctuation and messy organisation. Any task you put off becomes twice as hard when you go back to it. Spend 10 minutes checking over any piece of homework – an error in working out a maths problem could mean a change of grade, for example – before giving it in for marking.

Follow this four-point check when you have finished an essay or project:

1. Read through the question to remind yourself of the task.

2. Compare the finished piece with your plan, notes and research to check you have covered everything and have correctly transferred dates, numbers, quotes, names (double-check spellings) from your notes to your essay.

3. Read your homework to make sure you have provided a full answer, checking spelling and punctuation at the same time.

4. Have you written your name and form on each page and numbered the pages? Now, it's time to print out or produce the final copy!

GET REAL, PLEASE!

Once you've got a homework plan, here's how to make sure you stick to it:

Keep planning in proportion: Don't let your mission to devise the world's best ever homework plan become a way of avoiding work.

Be realistic: An ambitious plan that you ignore is much less use than a modest plan that you stick to closely.

Allow treats: Give yourself breaks every hour or so and have a work-free day on the weekend.

Negotiate with teachers: If you take charge of your work, your teachers will be pleased and will feel more positive towards your suggestions about homework.

CHAPTER 3

WHEN AND WHERE?

When and where you do your homework is going to have a huge effect on your attitude to homework and how successfully you do it. A one-page response to a drama question written while being bumped about on the noisy school bus is not going to be of the same standard as a piece thought about, planned and composed over a couple of nights while sitting comfortably and quietly at a desk. Cut the stress effect of homework by doing it when and where you feel most inspired and comfortable. Chances are this isn't on the school bus!

WHEN?

Between leaving school and going to bed there are many hours that you can fill with relaxation, socialising, sport, eating and drinking – and homework. How to get the best of work and play is the neat trick that is solved in this chapter.

DON'T DELAY FOR TV

You may need a moment or two to change out of your school clothes and raid the kitchen. But this is a critical moment. Fall prey to the black box and the entire late afternoon, early evening and night will disappear into a zillion pixels.

If a parent or carer is in when you come home, he or she may help you overcome the TV temptation. If you come home to an empty house it is harder to resist. But try!

ADVICE FROM THE TOP

Wise up and plan your TV viewing around your work – not the other way around.

USE THE TIMETABLE

If you know that you have a lighter workload some days, then you can take some time out of your homework schedule to do your own thing. Alternatively, you can take advantage of the 'easy' day to reduce the load for the next night.

This is not rocket science, it's just planning a little way ahead to make sure that you stay on top of homework without having to sacrifice favourite pastimes.

It is possible for you to go shopping, play five-a-side football or chat with friends **and** do your homework before the evening meal. This means that the rest of the evening is yours!

SOONER, NOT LATER

It's better to do tasks as soon as possible after the teacher has set them. They will be fresh in your mind, and you have a breathing space if the work turns out to be tougher than you anticipated.

Leaving it until the night before it's due in is not so clever. What if you find that other tasks have left you with too little time? What if you're given a ticket to a hot concert and have to refuse it because an assignment set a month ago is due the next day. Too bad!

If you check the homework assignment/task the day you get it and realise that you a) don't understand it, b) haven't a clue how to do it or c) haven't got the materials to do it, then you have time to go to the teacher and get it sorted! An extension may even be offered. But wait until the night before it's due and you'll get no sympathy from the teacher.

ADVICE FROM THE TOP

Even best friends who'll swim crocodile-infested rivers for you will be annoyed if you repeatedly ask them for homework help. Share-and-care runs out after six late night calls for the answers to the science quiz. You have been warned.

WORK AT SET TIMES

If you develop a routine of doing homework at set times, it will become automatic and you will not mind the loss of your time as much. Accepting that you do homework between certain hours also means that you won't let it take over an entire night. Better still, thoughts of undone homework won't ruin your free time.

Once the routine is established, then you can adapt it or be more flexible with it so that it fits in with things like a part-time job, babysitting, football practice or driving lessons.

DISTRACTING DEMONS

You know you are going to have do your homework sooner or later, so do it sooner and have the distractions later. Anything you use to put off work is a distraction – listening to music, watching TV or looking at a spider on the ceiling! When it comes to distracting demons, here are some of the worst offenders:

Phone calls: The friends who distract you by day do it again at night. If you have a mobile phone, turn it off while you work. Make an agreement that you will phone friends only at certain times, or that you will ring back if you still have homework to do.
Text messages can be used effectively to work together, but be careful – don't stray into personal chat.

43

Friends: There is nothing wrong with seeing your friends in the week; it's only a problem if that's all you do once the school gates close. If this is a familiar situation then it could mean that you're burning the midnight oil to do homework. Not a good idea and no one looks good with bags under their eyes!

At times, you may want to limit friends' visits to the weekend, especially if you are preparing for exams or end of key stage tests. If friends come to help you do homework, make sure this is what happens.

Activities: If you have an after-school activity you enjoy, don't give it up for your homework. But you may need to ask your teacher for permission to hand work in later than the date set for the rest of your class.

TV and music: Some pupils believe that they work better with the TV on or CD blasting. In a tiny number of cases this may be true, and there are some organising jobs and art/craft tasks that are aided by listening to music. But the most successful students work without such distractions.

If you think you work better with the telly on, you are in denial. Test this by working for two weeks without the TV being on and see if you can do the work more quickly and if your marks improve.

ADVICE FROM THE TOP

 If you work efficiently, you will have more time to watch TV or listen to music properly. You would never take your homework to the cinema. So why mix it with TV? If there's something you must see, either do your work before it's on, or record it to watch later.

HOME AND AWAY HOMEWORK

It may be called homework, but nowadays home is not always the best place to do it. Perhaps you find it hard to do school work once you come home. Or perhaps you have to fit in with the needs of other family members. Space may be limited, or you may have noisy siblings.

Library

Any library should give you a quiet and warm place to work, with adults to point you to relevant reference books. There may even be computers hooked to the Internet.

After-school study centres

Many schools now have an arrangement for you to work after school hours. It's surprising how calm school seems when other people leave. If you are lucky, you may be able to work with some adult supervision.

In many cities and towns you will also be able to go to a separate study centre. This may be in a school or college, or based in a football club. The study centre should be free for you to use, and will have the right furniture and equipment.

Home

This is the obvious place for homework. Your learning is important, but other family members have their own lives and needs. So you may need to negotiate a homework space.

You may also need to work out some ground rules. If there is one computer, will you take turns to use it? Is it fair to play your music when you don't want to put up with your sister's? These are questions for you to answer as a family.

CHANGING ROOMS

If you have a room of your own, how can you make it a good place for homework? Think about rearranging it, so it's a place where you want to be and where you want to work.

Perhaps your table or desk should face a window, so you can enjoy looking out. Or maybe it should be nearer the radiator or further away, so you don't freeze or roast. Perhaps you should place the TV or stereo where you will not be tempted to switch them on while you work.

The essentials

Desk or table: A desk uses space more efficiently, as it will have some storage. You need a good writing surface and room to spread things out. Make sure that the desk is well lit. Keep a clear area to use for working on new tasks.

Lamp: Use desk and standard lamps to create different lighting moods and effects for different kinds of study. Make sure that you have good lighting for reading.

Whenever possible work under natural light and ask a parent to buy light bulbs or fluorescent tubes that are labelled 'full spectrum'. These lights most closely resemble natural light and will go some way to reducing eye strain and tiredness.

ADVICE FROM THE TOP

An anglepoise lamp is designed as a work light. The shaded bulb can be moved to almost any position via two jointed and sprung arms mounted on a sturdy base. Not the most exciting Christmas present, but so worth it!

Chair: This is the most important thing to get right. You cannot beat a good desk chair. It should have a padded seat, and be big enough for you – adjustable ones are best.

Bookshelves: You can never have too many shelves, though make sure that the things you use the most – calculator, glue, scissors, geometry gear, dictionary, for example – are within easy reach.

STOCKING UP

Tempting as it is to raid stationery outlets and stock up on scented pens and colourful pads, you can get an awful lot of stuff free. Lots of businesses give away freebie pens, pads, mouse mats and sticky notes to advertise their products. Collect these and ask adults to pass any they get onto you.

Diary or planner: Your school supplies one, but if you want to buy one yourself, get one that follows the school year (September to August), provides space for a timetable, and shows all the weeks in the year at a glance.

Notebooks and paper pads: Spiral bound notebooks (sometimes called reporter's notebooks) allow you to tear out temporary or silly stuff, while keeping important notes to copy for revision or assessed work.

Desk tidy: You may need several of these (though a mug, plant pot or glass jar work just as well) to hold pens and other easily misplaced bits.

Ink eraser: Some erasers dissolve washable ink but not permanent ink. To erase permanent ink you can use a correction fluid pen/roller/mouse. Most schools frown on their use at school and ban bottled correction fluid altogether.

Calculator: You may need two – a basic one and a scientific calculator.

Bookstand: Plastic ones are inexpensive, but worth their weight in gold when you're trying to take notes from a book that refuses to stay open.

Pinboard: Stick important notices (exam timetable, revision timetable, for example) and documents on this.

Sticky notes: Write reminders to yourself, use them in essay planning (write ideas onto each sticky note then arrange them in order) or list facts to learn and put them where you will see them. For example, write *le frigidaire* on a sticky and put it on the fridge.

Dictionary: You could have a small basic one for school, but you need a good dictionary for home. An encyclopaedic dictionary is best, as this includes proper nouns and you can use it to find meanings, synonyms (same meaning) and antonyms (opposite meaning).

For the low-down on computer and Internet essentials, see Chapters 6 and 7. And for the full text of homework essentials, go to: **learn.co.uk > Homework guide > Essential furniture and equipment**

CHAPTER 4

HOMEWORK THROUGH THE STAGES

No matter how efficiently a primary school prepares their year 6 group for year 7, the first year of secondary school still comes as a shock. Then, just before you become a totally cocky year 10 (homework routine sussed and KS3 tests behind you), the KS4 curriculum lets you know you've still got a thing or three hundred to learn!

To take the 'surprise!' out of homework in years 7-9 and 10-11, here's a rundown of what you can expect, what is expected of you and how best to deal with it.

KEY STAGE 3

In most schools, your homework in year 7 will increase a lot. Why? It is not because senior teachers have a cruel streak but that you now have numerous teachers giving you homework, as opposed to just one main teacher. Frightening!

Worry, not

Unless you start your homework as soon as school finishes and find the work enjoyable, you should **not** do more than the upper limit (see page 13). You should also plan to finish your homework an hour or more before going to bed. Not quite so frightening, after all.

ADVICE FROM THE TOP

Late nights might be all right at weekends, but in the school week you need early nights and plenty of sleep, especially in the first term of year 7.

How much is too much?

If your work regularly takes longer than your teacher has suggested, it could be because you are:

- working with the TV or radio on (see pages 45–46) or are being distracted by friends or family.

- being too careful, trying too hard and doing too much.

- mucking around getting 'ready' to do homework, rather than actually doing it.

ADVICE FROM THE TOP

It may be that your teacher expects too much within the set time. If you think this is the case, speak to him or her.

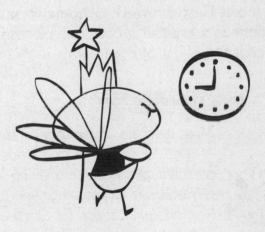

KEY STAGE 4

In Key Stage 4, your workload will increase enormously. If you can work with teachers to do assessment work that counts for more than one subject or category, this will help. For example, you might be able to present an English assignment as a piece of IT work that meets IT coursework or homework requirements. In other words, two pieces of work for the effort of one!

ADVICE FROM THE TOP

Most teachers advise that years 10 and 11 should be treated as one continuous course covering five terms. This is to encourage you to look and plan ahead for coursework and exams at the end of year 11.

Coursework

The coursework requirements for most subjects at GCSE and for other assessed courses such as Scottish qualifications are not excessive for work done over five terms. If you gradually build up your folders or portfolios, week by week, you will easily complete the work in time. If you need straightforward advice, read on.

Divide your time

- Don't work only on the subject you like, or in which (you think) you are doing well.

- Some subjects (maths and foreign languages, for example) need to be done for short periods but more frequently.

- English, history and art coursework, for example, benefit from longer periods of attention, less frequently.

ADVICE FROM THE TOP

Give yourself some breathing space by setting deadlines for big pieces of homework a couple of days before the real deadline. Use the extra couple of days before the 'real' deadline to read through the work and make final tweaks.

Organise your time

- Don't just live for the next deadline. If teachers relax the deadlines, don't put the work off any longer.

- Make sure you know the dates by which particular tasks are due, and final dates for all coursework.

- You cannot do all your coursework in the final term or two of year 11. If you try, you will be exhausted when you sit your exams and will under-achieve.

ADVICE FROM THE TOP

At the beginning of year 10 many schools ask you to select a teacher mentor. The mentor's job is to be there when you ask for help on anything related to your studies. If you're having trouble keeping on top of things, ask for advice now!

Less homework? Dream on!

Running parallel in years 10-11 with coursework and mocks and perhaps module tests is homework. You may think that the amount of homework you're getting is less, but this is a mirage. You are set fewer pieces of homework, but the 'size' of each piece has increased and so have the expectations of your teachers. When the guidelines suggest 1.5–2.5 hours of homework a day, they mean it. Teachers are looking for homework of a consistently high standard, handed in on time. If you start to slip behind in homework, then the chances are you're falling behind in coursework as well.

No homework? Think again

There is no such thing as a homework-free night during the school week in years 10-11. If you haven't any homework to do, you should be revising or doing coursework. Don't wait to be reminded of this – your school and your teachers expect you to have learned about independent learning, self-motivation and forward planning. Sounds tough, but only if you put off the inevitable.

SPREADING IT AROUND

If you would like a parent to be better informed about homework, direct them to: **learn.co.uk > Homework guide > Homework through the curriculum**

Being supported by a parent in all your efforts at school and at home can be a real boost to your confidence and to your results. But the National Curriculum is, for most parents, a new and strange beast; it is wildly different to the education system they 'enjoyed'! If this is the case, share this book with a parent or log them onto the **learn.co.uk** site.

There are also some articles, written by parents and experts, on the homework and independent learning issue. You and your parents can read these by going to: **learn.co.uk > Homework guide > Further reading in The Guardian and Observer**

If you have a part-time job, check out: **learn.co.uk > Homework guide > Sixth form and college – starting.** Here you'll find out how many hours you are legally allowed to work and what can happen if paid work starts to interfere with your studies.

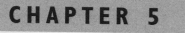

CHAPTER 5

GETTING THE JOB DONE - RIGHT!

Turning in a successful bit of homework consists of three parts: understanding the task, getting the content right and then presenting it in the best way. Miss out any of these and your marks will be affected.

Understanding the task: This is critical and consists of two things. The first is sussing the topic/subject/theme of the question. The second is spotting the keywords in the task that tell you how it should be done.

Content: Get stage one correct and everything that follows – planning, research, reading, learning, understanding, writing, problem-solving, etc. – will be on the right track.

Presentation: This is about handing in homework in the format requested, but also making sure it is a positive delight to your teachers.

RESEARCH

Assemble all your reference material – class books, textbooks, hand-outs, reference books, photostats, Internet downloads and print-outs. If it's a photocopy or electronic text, you may highlight things (with a pen or on screen). If it's a book, then jot things down in a notebook under a set of rough headings.

The 'rough' headings are created as a result of analysing the topic of the question/problem and deciding what information you need in order to provide a complete answer. It's vital to have a rough idea

of what you need before you start, otherwise an awful lot of research time could be wasted.

If you're not sure where to begin, then start with the following:

- Who was involved?
- What happened?
- When did it happen?
- Where did it happen?
- Why did it happen?
- How did it happen?

ADVICE FROM THE TOP

Cut research time by using the contents page and indexes to take you straight to the relevant information.

Make notes

When researching, don't forget you are
looking to satisfy both aspects of the task –
the topic and how it should be presented.
This may mean using graphs, evidence, data,
quotes, primary sources, etc. You could also be
instructed to compare, contrast, list, argue, for
example, or to present the findings as a
poster or brochure.

When you have gone through your reference material, make a second version of your notes. You might re-organise them in chronological order or in themes (population, economy, history, etc; aim, method, control, apparatus, etc.).

ADVICE FROM THE TOP

Use the right reading technique when there's lots to read. Scanning is running your eyes quickly down the page until you find the words you want. Skimming is when you read the first sentence of a paragraph to suss its content. If the first sentence relates to your search, then read the rest of the paragraph; if not, then keep skimming until you strike gold.

Clever spidergrams

A spidergram is useful when dealing with complex topics that involve many different but related aspects. At the centre write the topic of the project and around it write your main headings using arrows to show which are linked to which. Keep creating rings of sub-headings and linking them.

ADVICE FROM THE TOP

Write down the title and author of all sources, along with page numbers, website addresses, etc. Use a key to show which bits of research came from which sources. Statistics and data should be dated with the year they were gathered.

ESSAYS

Once your research is complete and your notes are organised, it's time to finalise an essay plan. Don't skimp on essay planning; give it as much time as you can – it won't be wasted.

An essay opens with an introduction and ends with a conclusion. Both are usually a paragraph in length. Between is the body of your essay where you use one paragraph for each idea. Within paragraphs, explain one point in one sentence.

ADVICE FROM THE TOP

Back up each idea or point whenever possible with a primary source – a quote or statistic, for example.

Teachers and examiners like to see each 'idea' being treated equally. If it is a 1500-word essay, don't use 750 words discussing your first idea then squeeze the other eight ideas and the conclusion into the remaining 750 words. Once you have your plan, divide the total word count between the introduction, body content and final conclusion.

ADVICE FROM THE TOP

Time and word limits should be followed. It is good practice for exams and prevents you doing too little or too much.

PROJECT OR COURSEWORK

These large pieces of work combine research and essay writing with spot-on presentation techniques. Present material as instructed in the task, but make sure your findings are easily understood and easily found. You don't want your teacher searching for the good stuff.

ADVICE FROM THE TOP

Look through some magazines or popular illustrated encyclopaedias and note how headings, text, illustrations and captions are used to get your interest and keep it. Projects and coursework should do the same.

Got to have a plan

For larger homework assignments, it is important to have a plan of work to ensure the following:

- you have covered all the material requested

- you know how you are going to start

- you know how you are going to finish

- you know how much work you have left to complete

- you know when you have completed your work

Take some time to complete a simple plan, and set yourself time limits for how long you spend on each section.

Signposts

A normal essay is not broken up by headings, but projects can be. Headings of different rank (large bold capitals for main headings; normal type for minor headings) and position (main ones centred, less important ones pushed to the left margin, for example) act as signposts, signalling each stage of your project. Your teacher can quickly scan these headings to get an overview of how successfully you have tackled the task.

Illustrations and tables of all kinds also act as signposts, but try to position them near the related text.

USE YOUR IMAGINATION

Here are five simple ideas that can make your project stand out from the rest. These can be achieved whether you are doing your project by hand or on a computer.

1. *Get it covered:* Design a cover page for your project with a strong and appropriate typeface for the title. A flowery italic script would suit a project on Elizabethan England, but not one on Stone Age civilisations. Add graphics to the cover – creepers and tendrils for a rainforest project, glittering stars for a solar system piece. For inspiration, check out book and magazine covers to see how they ignite your interest. But don't go over the top and don't spend days on it – you still have a project to research and write up!

2. *Heading in a different direction:* Headings usually run across the page, but you could run them down the right-hand edge. This works particularly well on big projects where each aspect occupies a page or more. The heading could be written/keyed into a coloured panel, with each panel a different colour.

ADVICE FROM THE TOP

Use the same colours to frame illustrations, tables or pictures to help link related information.

3. *Variety is the spice:* While it is not a good idea to use more than two fonts on a page (see page 118), add interest by using different types of illustrations – coloured and black-and-white, drawings and cartoons, maps and diagrams – and varying their size and shape. Instead of square or rectangular pictures, cut the image from its background (making sure the background doesn't contain something vital) and paste it onto the page. Use small graphics or pictures to decorate the start of a new section.

4. *Colour change:* Changing the colour of the typeface is not always successful. Pale type merges with the background; vibrant colours can literally vibrate giving you and your teachers a headache. Instead, try using coloured paper. Black type will stand out on most colours, and white type can be used on dark papers. Before committing to this, do some test pages and try to use coloured paper that relates to the topic.

5. *Text affects:* Great slabs of 'identical' text are very boring, so break them up with headings and illustrations. To get away from a repetitive heading-text-illustration routine, you can shorten the width of some sections of text and put an illustration alongside the text.

ADVICE FROM THE TOP

Do a rough plan of each page of your project showing where headings, text, pictures and captions need to be. Then tweak this plan to take in some imaginative presentation ideas.

HOW TO MAKE TEACHERS LOVE YOUR HOMEWORK

Although you will not be severely penalised if you have a genuine problem with your handwriting, it is essential that you take pride in the appearance of your work.

If you feel that good presentation is an optional extra, then consider it from your teacher's point of view. Messy, disorganised work can make marking hard work and if your teacher (or external examiner) can't decipher where you deserve marks, you won't get them.

Still not convinced that there are points in presentation? Then remember that you may have to read and takes notes from these same pieces of homework during test and exam revision. Karma or what?!?

Write-on tips

If you feel that your handwriting is costing you marks, try these tips:

- Write using black ink rather than blue (black type is easier to read).

- Write smaller (this requires more control and therefore you write more slowly).

- Each time you write, pick two letters and concentrate on forming those letters perfectly throughout. Pick two different letters the next time.

- Spoil yourself with some new writing gear, but don't just pick the snazziest; try the pens in the shop to find the one that encourages you to write neatly.

Ground rules

- Whether homework is presented on sheets of paper or in workbooks, date it and give it a heading.

- Make sure workbooks are named and show your form number. Do the same routine with homework on sheets of paper, but include name, form and date on every page and number every page.

- Most teachers prefer homework on A4-sized paper; ruled for handwritten work (unless it is a handwriting exercise) and plain for printed work. If a different format is wanted, teachers will tell you.

- Draw a margin (at least 2cm) on every page so there is room for your teacher to write comments.

- Don't staple pages together – it makes it hard to read. It is better to file your work in see-through, plastic sleeves or cardboard files. Avoid handing homework or assignments to teachers in ring binders as they are bulky to cart around.

- Computer software packages can help you create spectacular effects and designs, but remember that clarity is the most important thing. It pays to be conservative rather than flamboyant.

- Headings may be in bold and/or a larger type size, but should not be underlined, unless this is a style preferred by your school. Underlining has now come to represent a hyperlink.

- For large projects running over a few pages, it is helpful to include a contents page.

See also pages 115–124 in Chapter 7 for information about computer fonts, using pictures, templates and layouts.

HOW NOT TO BREAK A TEACHER'S HEART

Your teachers are desperate for you to do well in every aspect of your school career. It may not always seem like it, but they are on your side. They do, therefore, get angry when they have to mark your work down, ask for it to be done again or, more seriously, take the matter to a higher authority.

Here's how to be kind to your teachers
(and yourself!):

1. Don't do a rush job. You won't be fooling
   anyone.

2. Follow instructions and do what the
   'question' asks. Otherwise, your teacher will
   feel like he/she is wasting their time or that
   you care so little you couldn't be bothered
   to ask for help or do it correctly.

3. Check over all pieces of work before you hand them in.

4. If you quote from books or any other sources, enclose the quote in quote marks and state the source. If you 'copy' something and don't source it, it's called plagiarism and it's illegal. Teachers can take a complete sentence from your work and run it through a search engine. If the original text from which you copied is anywhere online, the search engine will find you out.

5. Work that you hand in must be your own. This is especially important for coursework that contributes to exam results. If you receive guidance from someone other than your teacher (for example, a parent, a friend, an expert on the topic), you must tell your teacher, who will record the nature of the assistance given to you.

6. Internet technology makes it possible to organise cheating online. Increasingly, students get chatting and organise essay swapping sessions or simply sell essays online. There is nothing clever about cheating. Once again, it's illegal.

7. Don't allow anyone to copy your work,
    especially any work you do for national
    exams or external marking. You and a
    friend can work together on research
    and swap ideas, but you must work
    independently on the final writing up. If
    two pieces of coursework are found to
    be identical or substantially the same, then
    both candidates can be disqualified from
    that subject and possibly other or all
    subjects. Serious stuff!

The law...

The good news is that you are allowed to copy things for school work as long as you acknowledge the source, don't make multiple copies, and if the copying has no significant economic effect on the copyright owner. So, do copy things for your school history project, but don't put them into magazines or sell them on to your friends.

For more information about being on the right side of the copyright law, go to: **www.intellectual-property.gov.uk/std/faq/ education/index.htm**

ADVICE FROM THE TOP

 Sometimes what you find on a site or in book is so well written that you can't see how to change it. One way is to make notes in your own words, delete or file the original text, and go back later to write your own version from your notes.

CHAPTER 6

COMPUTER WIZARDRY!

Have you ever wished for a friend who would help you do your homework? If you have access to a computer, then your wish can come true. You will earn a better grade and the work can be easier and much more fun with a computer. Is this too good to be true? Well, you still have to do SOME things for yourself, but in almost every area of school work, a computer will help you:

1. draft, revise and edit written work.

2. present work attractively.

3. explore and analyse different kinds of information.

4. gain access to Internet technologies.

5. save time.

Read it on-screen

If you want to find out more information about a particular topic – word processing, spreadsheets and calculators, pictures and printing – or want to read more about using a computer for homework, go to **learn.co.uk > Homework guide > Using your computer**

WHAT HARDWARE DO YOU NEED?

A basic PC (Personal Computer) or
Mac (Apple Macintosh) has lots of
bog-standard features, such as a modem
(connects a computer to a telephone line), a
disk drive, a monitor, and sometimes speakers.
To start with, all you need is a computer and
a printer. There are many things you might
want – a scanner, CD writer, digital camera or
DVD drive – but these are not essential and
can be added later.

ADVICE FROM THE TOP

*Macs have a reputation for being
easy to use, but Windows PCs are
less expensive for the same range
of features and are more common
in UK schools.*

WHAT PROGRAMS DO I NEED?

The National Curriculum says that you should be able to choose the appropriate software program for any task you are set. Here is a brief rundown of some of the options and their applications:

Program: Word processing
Application: For presenting information in writing and pictures and sending documents electronically
Examples: Microsoft Word, WordPad (comes free with Windows) and SimpleText

Program: Paint or Graphics
Application: For drawing and altering images
Examples: Paint (for PCs), Paintshop Pro, Graphic Converter

Program: Presentation graphics
Application: Used in business as a back-up to a speech or sales pitch. You can take it into the classroom to provide graphics, graphs, data, etc. to illustrate a spoken presentation
Examples: Microsoft PowerPoint, Lotus Freelance Graphics

Program: Spreadsheet
Application: To make data in tables more interactive for other users
Examples: Microsoft Excel, Lotus 1-2-3

Program: HTML Editor
Application: To create documents as web pages for online publication
Examples: Notepad or SimpleText (for raw coding), Dreamweaver, FrontPage

Program: Office Suite
Applications: : A complete package of programs including a word processor, spreadsheet, database and presentation graphics program
Examples: Microsoft Office Suite (educational discount of 60% available on the Student License Programme) or StarOfffice for PC, Appleworks for Mac

ADVICE FROM THE TOP

Get trial versions of software, or even full programs, by buying a computer magazine with a cover-mounted CD or DVD. You can also find free programs by searching online.

Your computer will almost certainly come with some basic programs and accessories – a simple word-processor, text-editor, calculator, file management and utilities to keep the system working well. It may also come with other applications already installed.

Get to know your machine

The first way to cut homework time down is to become totally familiar with what your computer can do:

1. Apply the skills used in IT classes – they really do work.

2. Refer to the user's guide for the programs you're using.

3. Be patient and practice regularly.

4. If you stumble across a really handy tool or short cut, write down where you found it and how to use it. Compile your own computer manual of short cuts and tips.

5. Keep your computer work organised and documents named.

6. Use your computer when researching, planning and drafting work.

7. Collect examples of neat presentation ideas.

8. Do a typing course online, at school or at an evening class.

What's on the menu?

When you start a new document (in Word, for example), the menu bar will appear at the top of the screen. Click on the menu items to see the Word commands. Here's a brief rundown of what's on the menu bar. (Some of these features are specific to Microsoft Word. Other word processors will have similar features, but may use different names and be found in different places.)

File: Useful for creating and saving files, and for opening existing files. When you make a new document, you will be shown a range of templates (see page 115) to choose from.

Edit: This menu has some of the simplest but most powerful functions, such as 'Cut', 'Copy' and 'Paste' (see page 116).

View: Most of us use 'Normal View' for ordinary work, but 'Outline View' should be used when you are reviewing and finishing a document. It lets you rank headings in order of importance (small, bold, italic, etc.), which in turn lets your teacher quickly see the structure of your essay or project. Try it out! 'View' also contains 'Toolbars and buttons'.

Insert: Use this for anything other than text in the main area of the page — pictures, text boxes, footnotes — and for a few other features, such as page numbering, headers, hyperlinks and symbols.

Format: Here you'll find fonts, text layout, bullet points, borders, indents, etc.

Tools: Go here for a word count, grammar and spell check, and to look up words in a dictionary or thesaurus.

Table: Use it to create a layout and to insert text into. 'Table AutoFormat' gives you options for styles and borders.

Short cuts

Your keyboard has over 100 keys, but only 26 are for letters of the alphabet. You can use the rest of the keys as short cut commands. On a PC, the Alt key plus a numeric keypad sequence will generate special characters (e.g. Alt +130 = é and on a Mac, Alt + e does the same thing). Even more useful are the Control/Commmand functions – Ctrl key on a PC; the 'apple' key on a Mac. For a complete list of speedy special characters, check out:

www.aardvarkusa.com/fun/altkeys.htm

For more about shortcuts, go to:
learn.co.uk > Homework guide > Using your computer – basics

Organise your files

The most important program on your computer is one many people rarely use, the file-management utility that helps you organise files. On recent versions of Windows this is Windows Explorer; on a Mac click on the Macintosh hardrive (HD) icon. It's a good idea to set up a 'folder' for each user of the computer. Inside your own folder, on 'sub folders' or 'files', save on-going coursework, assignments, subject notes and personal stuff.

Don't lose it

Most software programs automatically save work (Auto Save), but you should save it manually by choosing 'Save' on the File menu or by pressing 'Ctrl-S' (Command-S) or 'Apple - S'. Get into the habit of manually saving every couple of paragraphs. The first time you save a document, choose the 'Save As' option. Give the document a unique but logical name, and then specify where the document should be filed.

ADVICE FROM THE TOP

For different versions of an essay, use numbers to show the progression from research through drafts to copy ready for printing. For example, 'Mediastudy1.doc', 'Mediastudy2.doc'.

GETTING CLEVER

Templates

Many computer programs come with templates. Templates are files that contain some information (text or numbers) presented with a particular style and layout. These templates will help you to design professional-looking documents.

Each time you open a new document, a choice of templates is offered. You can also adapt and save an existing template to suit your purpose.

ADVICE FROM THE TOP

Whenever you create a template – either an original one or modify an existing one – give it a memorable name that clearly describes what it was used for.

Cut, copy, paste, action!

You'll find these powerful functions in the Edit menu. Together they let you move text within a document or from one document to another.

To cut, copy, paste:

1. Position the pointer at the start of the text you want to move.

2. Hold down the left mouse button (or sole button on some mice) and drag the pointer over the text to highlight it. Words can be highlighted by a double-click; a paragraph with a triple-click.

3. Go to the Edit menu and choose 'Cut' or 'Copy'.

4. Go back to the document you are working on and move the pointer to the new position. Go to 'Paste' on the Edit menu and the text will be pasted in the new position.

ADVICE FROM THE TOP

It is safer to use 'Copy' rather than 'Cut'. With 'Copy', the text stays in the original place as well as being pasted into the new position. Go back and delete the original text.

FONTS

The choice of typefaces is enormous and while it is fun mucking around with them, there are some guiding rules:

1. For work you are going to send on disk or electronically, stick to fonts such as Times New Roman, Arial and Verdana.

2. Try not to have more than two fonts on any page. Remember, though, that a font can be used in its roman, italic, bold and condensed forms, etc.

3. Good fonts for essay texts are: Times, Bembo, Courier, Arial and Helvetica in 12 or 14 point with 1.5 spacing between lines.

SPREADSHEETS

A spreadsheet is a document that contains information arranged into columns and rows. The spreadsheet program will analyse the information, sort it, perform calculations on it, present it in various formats and make charts to help you understand it.

You can use spreadsheets for almost any school subject – not just maths and science. For example, you can use a spreadsheet to create tables of information in history, and then sort it in different ways – a table of historical people could be sorted by date or alphabetically.

YOU CAN COUNT ON ME

Most computers have a calculator program included free with the operating software. On a PC with most Windows systems, it appears on the Programs menu, under 'Accessories'. On a Mac, look under the apple menu.

If you have a PC, click on 'View' and select between a simple calculator or a scientific one. Go to 'Help' on the file menu for tips.

ADVICE FROM THE TOP

You can find more advanced calculators on the Web if the free accessory on your computer is too limited. Try this download page: **www.topqualityfreeware.com/ calced.shtml**

PICTURE THIS!

Pictures should give important information which you cannot show in words – for example, a diagram to explain digestion or a detail from a famous painting. You can source your pictures:

... *off the web* – On a two-button mouse, use the right button to click on a picture and choose where you want the image to be saved. On a Mac, drag the picture to your desktop.

... *by creating your own* – Download digital photographs or scan printed images. A painting package (such as Paint for PCs) lets you create diagrams.

... by copying a screenshot to the clipboard or hard drive with special keys. For more about this and image editing go to:
learn.co.uk > Homework > Homework guide > Using pictures

To put a picture in a Word document, use the Insert menu, choose 'Picture', then 'From File...', and browse to the file you want.

Once the picture is on the page...

- position it near the relevant text

- crop (use only a part of the image) or resize for impact

- caption or label it

- use only one border design for framing

PRINTING

Most of the software you use will have a 'Print Preview' option. Don't print until you have adjusted margins so that everything (page numbers, for example) is inside the print area and that the page layout looks fine. When you print it's best to use the File menu and select 'Print' in order to bring up the dialogue box. This lets you choose what pages to print and how many copies, for example.

When printing draft copies:

- use the lowest quality setting

- use black ink

- use recycled paper

- print only a few pages at a time so you can make adjustments to the document after reading the draft

Only when you're 100% satisfied, go for the best quality paper and high print quality for your final printout.

HEALTHY YOU

Using your computer is more pleasant if you take care of some simple things.

- *Monitor* – It shouldn't flicker and the contrast and brightness levels should be adjusted to suit. Sit an arm's length away from the monitor. Raise your sitting position so that you look down towards the screen, rather than looking up or straight at it.

- *Desk* – The keyboard and mouse pad should be on the same surface.

- *Posture* – Make sure your legs feel comfortable and if your feet don't reach the floor, get a footrest. Sit with your back upright, your arms bent at the elbow and wrists straight. Avoid bending and twisting your neck.

- ***Don't use force*** – Type lightly, mouse-click gently and hold the mouse in a relaxed grip.

- ***Look after your eyes*** – Blink often and make sure you look away from the screen regularly.

- ***Take a break*** – Every half hour you should get up and go for a short walk, make a drink, go to the toilet, etc.

CHAPTER 7

NET ATTRACTION

The Internet lets you use a number of different technologies that can help you with homework – two of these are particularly good: the Web and email.

The Web: The World Wide Web is a vast source of information on the Internet. It's like having the world's largest library on your desk. The web is constantly being updated and is continually expanding.

Email: Using a computer connected to the Internet, you can exchange messages with other Internet users across the world or next door. This can be particularly helpful for foreign language practice or asking teachers and other students for help with homework.

All the information in this chapter can be accessed on-screen if you go to: **learn.co.uk > Homework guide > Using the Internet**

IT'S A MODEM WORLD

The crucial bits of gear for Internet and email is a modem and a telephone line. Some computers come with an in-built modem; others have a separate modem unit. Both do the job of letting your computer access the Internet via the telephone line.

To look at web pages, you need a web browser. These are programs that are loaded onto the computer that help you find documents, read them, save them and go back to them. Two of the most popular are Netscape Navigator and Internet Explorer. You may have one of these programs or both.

To use the Internet, you first need a service provider. Some of these give a service that is 'free', apart from the cost of your phone calls. If you are a frequent user, then you may prefer a service that gives you unlimited Internet access for a fixed monthly rental.

PORTALS AND ENGINES

It is easy to waste time online, but to find things quickly you will rely on two kinds of tools – portals and search engines.

A portal (Latin for a door or gate) is like a library or directory. It organises things into categories, then smaller sub-categories. You will usually find something on the subject you are looking for, but not everything, as the portal will list only a limited number of websites.

Portals vary – there is not one that is obviously the best for everything. 'Yahoo' **(www.yahoo.com)** has been the most successful in marketing itself. 'About' **(www.about.com)** perhaps has the best coverage for school-type work.

A search engine is a very different kind of tool. It uses brute strength to look at millions of pages, and is able to select those sites that contain your keywords. If you are looking for something very unusual, then you will probably start with a search engine. If you are looking for something on which there is lots of information, then a portal may help you find resources of better quality.

For school, college and university work, the best search engine to use is 'Google' (**www.google.com**). Microsoft's Internet Explorer has a search facility – and you can reset it to use 'Google' or another search engine of your choice. Many people simply click the Explorer 'search' button, and accept the search engine Microsoft uses, but this may not always be the best one.

JUST BROWSING

Web browsers can help you find what you want. Begin to type in a web address and the latest browsers will try to complete it for you. Click the down arrow to the right of the address bar to see a drop-down list of sites. Add sites you like to your 'favourites' or 'bookmarks'.

Use 'back' and 'forward' arrows to see earlier or later pages. Use 'home' to go to your home page. To set your own choice of home page – go to 'Tools' then 'Internet Options' in Internet Explorer or 'Edit' then 'Preferences' in Netscape Navigator.

To increase the page size in Internet Explorer (not in Netscape) press F11. Press it again to change back.

Plug me in

Plug-ins are 'freeware' programs that extend what your browser does. You need them for multimedia, sound and animation. Usually, you will be prompted to download a plug-in if you don't already have it.

HYPERDRIVE HYPERLINKS

Clicking on a hyperlink causes your browser to open a new page. If the 'back' arrow is greyed out, the browser has opened a new window. Browsers underline hyperlinks by default, and change the colour of visited or active links. Hyperlinks can also be found in images or even areas of images (image maps). When your mouse pointer moves over a hyperlink, it will turn into a hand graphic.

SAVING PAGES

Web pages are kept in small files, so you can save lots, even on a floppy disk. Your browser lets you choose whether to keep images and other files included in the page. If you just want the words, then you can save them as a text file (this removes the HTML code).

When it comes to printing from the web, it may be better to copy the information and put it into another document. By default, a printer will show, as a footer, the address of the web page – even if it's on your hard drive. This can help you find it later. If you use the File menu for printing, you will see a print dialogue, which lets you choose what to print. This is helpful if you are printing from a site with frames. (You can also right click in a frame, and choose 'Print' from the menu.)

COOL SURFING

1. Learn to be critical about what you read on the Web. There are some great sites that are 100% reliable and then there are the rest. To decide how reliable a site is, you need to look at who wrote it, what kind of authority the site has, and who else recommends it.

2. It's easy to get lost on the Web. Unless you are definite about what you are looking for, you'll be tempted to wander off in all directions. This can be fun and what you find might be absolutely fascinating though totally useless. Write down what you're looking for and stick to it!

3. learn.co.uk is a highly reliable source of everything to do with the National Curriculum. On this site you will find lessons, tests, resources, revision guides, special topics and hyperlinks to thousands of websites that will deliver what you need for homework, assignments and coursework for KS1 through to A-level.

4. It's ever so easy to spend too much time on your computer. Try to take breaks from your computer, and give yourself a computer-free day each week.

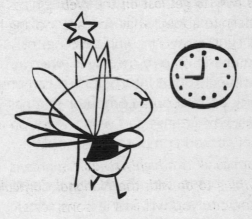

YOU HAVE EMAIL

Use email to discuss things with friends, or to send work to your teacher. Putting things briefly into an email message will help you think more clearly.

- You can send email using programs on your computer (such as Outlook Express, Eudora and Netscape Messenger). These programs work offline – for reading, sorting, answering and deleting mail. You send and receive messages when you connect to the Internet. They can only pick up mail on a computer that has your mailbox settings and won't work on a networked computer at school.

- Web-based mail allows you to send and read messages by using a website. Its disadvantage is that you can't use it offline.

The most well known is Hotmail, but many
schools and colleges block this because it
has been used a lot to distribute viruses
and pornography.

• Some mail services will let you use a
  program on your computer to pick up
  mail and give you access on the Web.
  A service that lets you do this is the
  personal mail provided by 'UKOnline'
  (**www.ukonline.co.uk**).

Sending an email

Send messages as plain text, rather than Word
or HTML files. This travels more quickly and
ensures other users can read your message.
It is fine to send attachments (a small JPEG
image file or a document file) that are useful
with your homework. It is not a good idea to
send your friends emails with 10Mb worth of
media files, which take hours to download.
Your friends may set up their machine to
block your mail.

Learn to clip and
edit mail when
you reply. Decide
whether your
comments should all
go at the top, or be
mixed in with the
original message.

Chat time

Some adults worry about chat, but it is simply a system for sending messages in real time. Many young people use chat to hang out, read what others have written and... chat! You can also get help with school work if you're in a homework or revision-type chat room. If you can't find one that's right, then why not start a chat group with your schoolmates?

SAFE CHAT

Most scare stories about the Internet are misinformed and exaggerated – you are in far more danger from traffic on the road to school, than from people who want to stalk you online. This guide to Internet safety is adapted from NCH's NetSmart Rules for safe surfing on the net. For the full details, go to: www.nch.org.uk/itok

Never...

... tell anyone you meet on the Internet your name, home address, your telephone number or your school's name, unless a parent/carer specifically gives you permission.

... send anyone your picture, credit card or bank details, or anything else without first checking with a parent/carer.

... give your password to anyone, even a best friend.

... arrange to meet anyone in person without first agreeing it with a parent/carer, and get them to come along to the first meeting, which should be in a public place.

... open attachments to emails unless they come from someone you already know and trust.

... respond to nasty, suggestive or rude emails or postings in chat rooms.

Always...

... keep your password to yourself, do not share it with anyone.

... check with your parent/carer that it is OK to be in a chat room.

... be yourself and do not pretend to be anyone or anything you are not.

... remember – if someone makes you an offer which seems too good to be true, it probably is.

HYPER CRITICAL

The Internet is a wonderful source of information, but just as you would be critical about information found in books, newspapers, magazines, on television or radio, or picked up from friends, you must be equally choosy about what you pick up on the Internet. It is also critical that you convert what you discover on websites into notes, written in your own words, that you understand.

SIGNING - OFF!

Now that you have sussed the quickest and smartest ways through your homework, picked up some planning and presentation tips and learned how to get ace marks without staying up all night, what are you going to do with your free time?

The first thing you can do is disappoint those researchers who say you'll simply curl up for hours and hours in front of the television. The second thing you can do is indulge yourself with your favourite pastimes. There's a lot of truth in the saying: 'All homework and no play makes Jack/Jill one major bore'. Put some air under the wheels of your skateboard or aim for a personal best on the track or in the pool. Get together with friends for idle gossip or curl up with a good book. Learning to enjoy a really healthy balance between work and play is a skill for life!

CHAPTER 8

RESOURCES

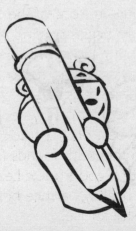

On the following five pages are web addresses or phone numbers for homework help and freephone counselling services.

Homework help online

learn.co.uk can be used for homework throughout the National Curriculum and also hosts an 'Ask a maths teacher' service.
www.learn.co.uk

learn.co.uk's Web guide has over 1,000 links to websites that can help you with your homework.
www.learn.co.uk/webguide/

The Association of Teacher Websites has links to websites made by teachers.
www.byteachers.org.uk/

For links and reviews of good education resources on the web, go to:
www.schoolzone.co.uk/

www.topmarks.co.uk/

Channel 4's Homework High site is an 'Ask a teacher' service.
www.homeworkhigh.com/

Homework via email

If you can send homework to your school electronically, your school may already have a secure storage which will protect your homework from being 'stolen' or read by other students. If not, you can find such services free on the web by going to:
MyVisto: **www.myvisto.com**

Smartgroups: **www.smartgroups.com**

Online reference books

Encyclopaedias:
Encarta Encyclopaedia: **www.encarta.msn.com**

Columbia Encyclopaedia:
www.bartleby.com/65/

Encyclopaedia.com:
www.encyclopedia.com

Dictionaries:
The Oxford English Dictionary: **www.oed.com**

Ask the experts at Oxford Dictionaries:
www.askoxford.com

Onelook dictionary portal: **www.onelook.com**

Academic Info's big list of dictionary sites:
www.academicinfo.net/refdictionaries.html

Atlases and maps:
Multimap: **uk.multimap.com**

GeoStar (Shell site): **www.shellgeostar.com**

Mapquest (US site): **www.mapquest.com**

Outline maps: **www.maps.com** or
**geography.miningco.com/library/maps/
blindex.htm.**

Freephone counselling services

Childline
Tel: 0800 1111
www.childline.org.uk/

Samaritans
Tel: 08457 90 90 90
jo@samaritans.org
www.samaritans.org.uk/

Safe surfing and cool computing

Internet safety: www.safety.ngfl.gov.uk/

IBM's Healthy Computing:
www.pc.ibm.com/ww/healthycomputing

Ergonomics for kids:
www.healthycomputing.com/kids

Working in Comfort: www.hp.com/ergo HP's

NCH's NetSmart Rules: www.nch.org.uk/itok

WANT TO KNOW MORE?

Look out for these other titles developed in association with **learn.co.uk:**

Top Websites for Homework
by Kate Brookes
The first ever pocket guide to the best websites for homework. More and more students are using the Internet as a rich source of information for their homework. This book provides you with an invaluable shortcut to dozens of the most useful websites. All you have to do is look up the school subject, and take your pick. Addresses and short descriptions are provided for each recommended site.

Revision Sorted! by Kate Brookes
Life saving revision tips in a handy format.
Every student at some point has to face up
to the ghastly reality of EXAMS. This book
staves off panic and confusion with its calm
and practical advice, on everything from
revision plans and methods to stress-busting
strategies and top exam techniques. All
presented in easily digestible chunks and a
reassuring style – SORTED!

Other titles by Hodder
Children's Books

the txt book by Kate Brookes
The best text message book ever!
All the abbreviations, acronyms and similes
you will ever need, together
with lots of hints on expert
texting. Packed with essential
messages for all aspects of life,
together with a few to make
you giggle...

Little Book of Exam Skills by Kate Brookes
Prepare yourself for exams with this little
book. It's packed with brilliant revision tips you
can start using *right now* – plus top exam
techniques to help you make the grade!

Little Book of Exam Calm by Anita Naik
Keep your cool at exam time with the help of
this little book. Packed with advice on how to
stay happy and healthy before and during
your exams, it will provide you with a calm
and confident route to exam success!

You can buy all these books from your local
bookseller, or order them direct from the
publisher. For more information, write to:

The Sales Department, Hodder Wayland,
a division of Hodder Headline Limited,
338 Euston Road, London, NW1 3BH.

Visit our website at
www.madaboutbooks.com